MACHINES RULE

ON THE ROAD

Steve Parker

FRANKLIN WATTS
LONDON•SYDNEY

This edition 2012

First published in 2008
by Franklin Watts

Copyright © Franklin Watts 2008

Franklin Watts
338 Euston Road
London NW1 3BH

Franklin Watts Australia
Level 17/207 Kent Street
Sydney, NSW 2000

Editor: Jeremy Smith
Design: Billin Design Solutions
Art director: Jonathan Hair

A CIP catalogue record for this book
is available from the British Library.

Dewey number: 629.222

Printed in China

ISBN 978 1 4451 0929 9

Picture credits: Aston Martin: 6, 10, 11r,
11br. Bruce Benedict/Transtock/Corbis:
11b. Bugatti: POFC, 4-5, 8-9. Ducatti:
19c & b. istockphoto: OFC bl & br, 7t,
7c, 7b, 12 all, 13t, 13b, 22 all, 23t,
23b, 24 all, 25c.
www.JayOhrberg.com: 13c.
Shutterstock: 11t, 14b, 14t, 15c, 15b,
16, 17 all, 19t, 20-21 all, 23tr, 25 all,
26-27 all, 28-29 all, 30-31 all.

Franklin Watts is a division of
Hachette Children's Books,
an Hachette UK company.

www.hachette.co.uk

CONTENTS

Words in bold appear in the glossary at the back of the book.

Highway fever

Beautiful scenery, wide views, wonderful sights, and a surge in engine power – travelling the open road is great fun.

Some people zoom along in supercars and saloons, while others roar off on motorbikes. Larger vehicles such as **limousines** and tour buses carry groups of people, while lorries bring stuff to the shops for us. Finally, gritters and other heavy vehicles are needed to keep the roads working for everybody.

Cars

Cars are the most popular form of transport in the world. Saloons carry people along in comfort and luxury, while amazing supercars can whizz along at great speeds.

Party vehicles

When lots of people want to travel together, bigger vehicles are needed! Stretch limousines and buses can both carry many people at once in luxury.

Heavy vehicles

We all rely on the food and other goods that big vehicles like lorries can carry. Other larger machines help to shift snow, fill in holes and make sure that the roads stay safe for everybody to use.

Motorbikes

Whether dodging through city traffic or out on the open road, two wheels is often the fastest way to travel.

Supercar

The fastest cars in the world are called supercars. The Bugatti Veyron is the quickest and most expensive supercar in the world today. Bugatti have decided that only 300 Veyrons will ever be made.

This new Bugatti is named after French racing driver Pierre Veyron, who won the 24-hour Le Mans race in 1939 while driving for Bugatti.

engine bay

spoiler

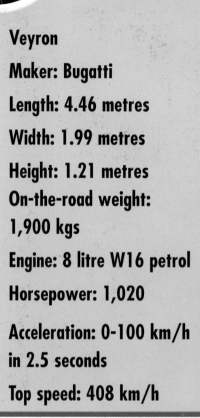

THAT'S INCREDIBLE

If your Bugatti needs to be repaired, a mechanic has to be flown in specially. Bugatti promise somebody will be available 24 hours a day.

Stats and Facts

Veyron

Maker: Bugatti

Length: 4.46 metres

Width: 1.99 metres

Height: 1.21 metres
On-the-road weight: 1,900 kgs

Engine: 8 litre W16 petrol

Horsepower: 1,020

Acceleration: 0-100 km/h in 2.5 seconds

Top speed: 408 km/h

steel instrument panel

To reach speeds above 370 km/h, the driver needs to use a special 'Top Speed' key (left). When the key is inserted, the spoiler retracts, and the car drops to less than seven centimetres off the ground. This makes the car more streamlined and able to go even faster.

Luxury saloon

Fast, safe, quiet and comfortable, the luxury saloon car is the finest way to ride the roads. With all the latest gadgets, from satellite navigation to air-conditioning, the longest journeys simply fly by.

V12 AML

The Aston Martin Vanquish is a grand tourer first sold in 2001. The Vanquish S is the fastest car ever made by Aston Martin. It can roar to speeds over 320 km/h.

THAT'S INCREDIBLE

The car's the star for the Vanquish. It features in several movies such as James Bond's *Die Another Day* and *Lara Croft: Tomb Raider*.

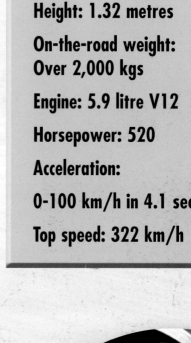

cylinders

The Vanquish has a **'V' engine**. 'V' engines have two rows or banks of cylinders at an angle, forming a 'v' shape.

sat nav screen

Vanquish S

Maker: Aston Martin

Length: 4.67 metres

Width: 1.92 metres

Height: 1.32 metres

On-the-road weight: Over 2,000 kgs

Engine: 5.9 litre V12

Horsepower: 520

Acceleration:

0-100 km/h in 4.1 seconds

Top speed: 322 km/h

Luxury saloon car makers, like Aston Martin, Jaguar and BMW, make sure the driver can see and reach everything easily, including the **sat nav** screen.

*Smooth **alloy** wheels*

Stretch limo

Big luxury cars can be made
even larger by stretching them longer into a stretch
limousine. Then you can fit in ten people or more, and
have a party on the road!

This is a stretch Hummer, the road version of the US big military jeep called the Humvee.

THAT'S INCREDIBLE

Jay Ohrberg has made lots of other limos, including a Ferrari limo and several batmobiles.

Stats and Facts

The longest **limousine** in the world was built by Jay Ohrberg. The 'American Dream' was made by cutting up and putting back together four Cadillacs. The result was a limo over 30 metres long with room for a helipad on the end!

Longest stretch limo

Maker-owner: Jay Ohrberg

Length: 30.5 metres

Wheels: 26

On-the-road weight: 10-plus tonnes

Features: Jacuzzi tub, pool with diving board, satellite TV, kingsize waterbed, sun deck, helipad

Body: Can be rigid or hinged in the middle for cornering

Drivers: 2, front and rear (to help reversing)

Uses: Movies and exhibitions (it's too long for roads)

luxury interior

On-road, off-road

ATVs are All-Terrain Vehicles like quad bikes, able to travel almost anywhere. SUVs are Sports Utility Vehicles, stylish and powerful yet tough and rugged. With the press of a button all four wheels are driven by the engine (4WD mode). This makes these vehicles able to tackle dirt tracks and cross-country trips.

The quad bike is like a four-wheeled motorbike. It can bounce over stones and zoom up steep slopes, but it needs skill to steer. It is also best to wear a crash helmet!

THAT'S INCREDIBLE
In 2004 Graham Hicks rode a quad bike at 213 km/h — and he is blind and deaf!

Stats and Facts

Range Rover

Maker: Land Rover

Length: 4.97 metres

Width: 2.19 metres

Height: 1.90 metres

On-the-road weight: 2,600 kgs

Engine: Supercharged

4.2 litre V8 petrol

Horsepower: 390

Acceleration: 0-100 km/h in 7.5 seconds

Top speed: 210 km/h

SUVs such as Range Rovers can drive over all kinds of terrain, from ordinary roads up to unmade, rocky tracks.

gear knob

Many SUVs have **automatic transmission**. The car changes **gear** by itself. The button on the side of the gearstick here puts the car into **4WD** mode.

good grip

Tour bus

When singers, music bands, sports teams and theatre groups go 'on the road', they travel from place to place, night after night in a luxury tour bus. They relax or practise, chat or doze, ready for the night's big performance.

The gleaming tour bus is a hotel on wheels. It is fully equipped with food, drinks, music, DVDs and other needs for the hard-working performers.

Stats and Facts

band relaxing

luxury leather seats

Typical luxury tour bus

Maker: Various

Length: 12-16 metres

Width: 2.5 metres

Height: 4 metres

On-the-road weight: 6-10 tonnes

Engine: V8 diesel

Horsepower: 500-plus

Features: Armchairs, sofa, big screen satellite TV and DVD, music system, bunk beds, snacks and drinks bar, toilet, shower, climate control ...

THAT'S INCREDIBLE

Featherlite Luxury Coaches have just launched the most expensive luxury bus in the world. Each one costs nearly $3 million!

This luxury coach transports tourists all across Australia. It can travel for over a thousand kilometres without having to refuel.

Sports bike

The sports bike is king of the open road. It can roar away like a rocket, reach the speed limit in just a few seconds, and lean into bends at breathtaking pace.

Surging into a bend, the rider tilts into the curve as the sides of the tyres keep their grip. The front and rear **disc brakes** are ready for instant use.

suspension forks

THAT'S INCREDIBLE

The world land speed record for two wheels was set by Chris Carr in 2006 at 562 km/h, in a specially designed motorbike that looks more like a rocket!

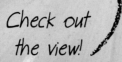

Check out the view!

Stats and Facts

Ninja ZX-14

Maker: Kawasaki

Length: 2.16 metres

Width: 0.76 metres

Height: 1.17 metres

On-the-road weight: 220 kgs

Engine: 1.35 litre 4 cylinder petrol

Horsepower: approx 200

Acceleration: 0-100 km/h in 3 seconds

Top speed: 300 km/h (limited)

exhausts

cylinder

This sports bike has two cylinders. You can see the exhaust pipes coming out of the cylinder.

Cruising bike

Cruising bikes may not be the fastest motorbikes, but they are powerful and comfortable for long rides. Bikes such as this Harley-Davidson also look very cool with all that chrome!

mudguards

Cruising bikes have the engine low down and the wheels far apart, which is called a long **wheelbase**. Mudguards are important if it rains!

Stats and Facts

FXDI Dyna Super Glide

Maker: Harley-Davidson

Length: 2.36 metres

Wheelbase: 1.63 metres

Seat height: 0.67 metres

Fuel tank: 18 litres

On-the-road weight: 300 kgs

Engine: 1.44 litre V2 petrol

Transmission: 6-speed gearbox

In a disc brake, pads press on the ring-shaped disc attached to the wheel.

dial shows road speed

dial shows engine turning speed (rpm)

THAT'S INCREDIBLE

The Harley-Davidson Motor Company's bikes are ridden by police around the world and have starred in countless movies.

Bikers meet up and show off their latest motorbikes.

Road train

Road trains are huge vehicles with massively powerful diesel engines. They get their name because they pull along a string of trailers just like a train has to pull carriages along.

Road trains pull trailers carrying all kinds of goods, from metal containers to machinery, tanks of fuel and drums of chemicals.

Stats and Facts

Australian road trains

Maker: Mack, Kenworth, Cummins, Volvo and others

Trailers: Usually doubles, triples or quads (up to 4)

Double length: 35 metres

Double weight: 80 tonnes

Triple length: 53 metres

Triple weight: 120 tonnes

Speed limit: 90 or 100 km/h depending on state

Livestock, such as cows and sheep, travel in special trailers. They must be fed and given water every few hours.

THAT'S INCREDIBLE

In 2006 the longest Australian road train had a Kenworth **tractor unit** and 112 trailers. It was 1,475 metres in length, and weighed over 1,000 tonnes!

These trucks are taking a rest from the blazing heat.

Snow plough

On the road, snow means slow! As the snow falls it reduces the distance that drivers can see. As the snow settles, it becomes slippery and crunchy. So send for the snow plough!

The **snow plough** is a powerful truck with an angled blade at the front that pushes the snow to one side.

plough blades

HD Series snow plough blade

Suitable for: 4WD trucks of about one tonne

Maker: Fisher

Blade length: 2.75 metres

Ploughing width:

2.44 metres

Height: 0.73 metres

Weight: 330 kgs

Construction: 11 gauge steel

Strengthening ribs: 8

After the snow plough has passed, the centre of the road is almost clear. But cars caught in the first flurry of snow remain stuck at the sides.

snow chains

high-grip tread

The snow blower has a powerful fan to blow the snow a long way, so it does not pile up in a long ridge.

THAT'S INCREDIBLE
One of the biggest snow plough blades is 9.8 metres wide and 1.2 metres tall, and is used to clear snow from airport runways.

Road makers & menders

To drive a sports car or sports bike on the road, you need a good road to drive on! An army of road-making machines build smooth, flat streets and wide highways so we can travel in safety and comfort.

caterpillar tracks

bucket

To make a road, massive long-reach diggers with **caterpillar tracks** and wide buckets start to clear the area.

Then a wide-scoop digger scrapes the ground level, often helped by a bulldozer.

Stats and Facts

The first tarmac road was laid in Paris in 1854.

In the USA alone there are 3 million kilometres of surfaced roads, which would stretch to the Moon and back four times.

Australia's Highway 1 goes around the edge of the country and is the world's longest national highway, at more than 20,000 km.

Chippings are pressed down by a compactor.

A hot tar spreader lays the asphalt.

A road-roller squeezes the asphalt flat.

Glossary

4WD

Four-wheel-drive, where the engine turns all four wheels.

Alloy

A combination or mixture of metals. or of metals and other substances, such as stainless steel.

ATV

All-Terrain Vehicle, a car or quad bike or similar that can cross the roughest ground.

Automatic transmission

When a vehicle changes gear by itself, according to its speed and load, and the roughness and steepness of the ground.

Caterpillar track

A 'crawler' or long ridged belt in a loop shape that goes round and round, with wheels inside it, as used on tanks and big construction vehicles.

Disc brakes

Brakes which work by two pads fixed to the vehicle pressing on a ring-shaped disc that rotates with the roadwheel.

Exhaust

The pipes and tubes that carry the burned waste gases away from a petrol or diesel engine.

Gears

A system of cogs or wheels inside a gearbox that allows a vehicle to go at different speeds without stressing the engine.

Limousine

A large, long luxury car.

Road train

A truck that pulls a line of trailers.

Sat nav

Satellite navigation, finding the way using signals from GPS (Global Positioning System) satellites high in space.

Snow chains

Metal chains that fit over a tyre to give a better grip when driving over snow or ice.

Snow plough

A powerful truck with an angled blade at the front that pushes the snow to one side.

Suspension

The springs, pistons, levers and other parts that soak up bumps and hollows in the ground, so the people in a vehicle have a smooth ride.

SUV

Sports Utility Vehicle, a tough, strong vehicle that can do many jobs.

Tractor unit

The cab and engine part of a big articulated truck.

Tread

On a tyre, the surface pattern of grooves and bumps.

V engine

An engine with two rows or banks of cylinders at an angle, forming a 'v' shape.

Wheelbase

The distance between the axles of a vehicle, from the centre of the front wheel to the centre of the rear wheel.

Find out more

http://www.howstuffworks.com/engine.htm
Explanations about how vehicle engines and their parts work.

www.2sportscars.com/
Pictures and descriptions of all kinds of sports cars and other fast cars.

http://trucks.about.com/od/specialtytrucks/Classic_Trucks_and_Other_Specialty_Trucks.htm
Every kind of truck, big and small, along with trucking history, monster trucks and much more.

http://www.classicbikedashboard.com/
A huge site with more than 120 makes of motorbikes.

Further reading

Diggers and Cranes (Usborne Big Machines) by Caroline Young, Chris Lyon, and Teri Gower, Usborne 2006

Go Turbo: Custom Cars by Jim Brush, Franklin Watts 2011

Go Turbo: Hot Bikes by Roland Brown, Franklin Watts 2009

Motor Mania series by Penny Worms, Franklin Watts 2010

Note to parents and teachers:

Index